M000012564

To:

From:

peace

COMPILED BY
Lois Kaufman

INTRODUCTION BY
Barbara Paulding

PETER PAUPER PRESS, INC.
WHITE PLAINS, NEW YORK

Designed by David Cole Wheeler

Copyright © 2009
Peter Pauper Press, Inc.
202 Mamaroneck Avenue
White Plains, NY 10601
ISBN 978-1-59359-772-6
Printed in China
7 6 5 4 3 2 1

Visit us at www.peterpauper.com

peace

The sweetest song is the song of peace, as it sings through the soul and finds a place in the world. Peace manifest may require understanding, work, harmony, freedom, and justice, but it begins with the quiet mind and pervasive love. This little volume honors insights from poets, prophets, and everyday folk.

Peace be with you.

Peace puts forth buds
in the full fruitfulness
of Truth.

HILDEGARD OF BINGEN

This is the way of peace:
Overcome evil with good,
falsehood with truth,
and hatred with love.

You cannot find peace anywhere
save in your own self....
When a man has made peace
with himself, he will be able to
make peace in the whole world.

RABBI SIMHA BUNAM

I do not want the peace
which passeth understanding,
I want the understanding
which bringeth peace.

HELEN KELLER

True and lasting
inner peace can never be
found in external things.
It can only be found within.
And then, once we find and
nurture it within ourselves,
it radiates outward.

AUTHOR UNKNOWN

God blesses peace
and curses quarrels.

MIGUEL DE CERVANTES

The mind is never right
but when it is at peace
within itself.

LUCIUS ANNAEUS SENECA

The peaceful are the strong.

OLIVER WENDELL HOLMES

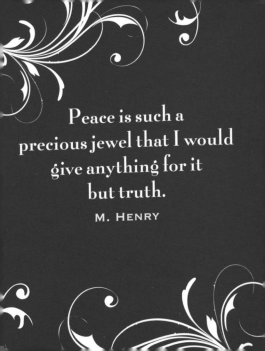

Peace is such a
precious jewel that I would
give anything for it
but truth.

M. HENRY

In quietness and confidence
shall be your strength.

ISAIAH 30:15

Peace is the fairest form
of happiness.

WILLIAM ELLERY CHANNING

Peace is not a passive but
an active virtue.

FULTON J. SHEEN

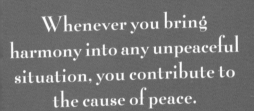

Whenever you bring
harmony into any unpeaceful
situation, you contribute to
the cause of peace.

PEACE PILGRIM

If the pursuit of peace is both old and new, it is also both complicated and simple. It is complicated, for it has to do with people, and nothing in the universe baffles man as much as man himself.

ADLAI STEVENSON

Peace is better
than a fortune.

ST. FRANCIS DE SALES

I harmonize with nature
and all others in my world.
I accept greater peace
in my life now.
And so it is.

DIANE DREHER

Peace is better than
a place in history.

JUSTO PASTOR BENITEZ

Peace comes to us
through love, understanding
of our fellow men, faith.
Peace does not include
selfishness nor indifference.
Peace is never wrapped
at a counter for a price.
It is earned by giving
of ourselves.

ANNETTE VICTORIN

We do not want riches,
we want peace and love.

RED CLOUD

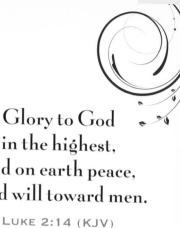

Glory to God
in the highest,
and on earth peace,
good will toward men.

LUKE 2:14 (KJV)

Peace is a daily, a weekly,
a monthly process, gradually
changing opinions, slowly eroding
old barriers, quietly building
new structures. And however
undramatic the pursuit of peace,
that pursuit must go on.

JOHN FITZGERALD KENNEDY

The first and fundamental
law of nature is to seek peace
and follow it.

THOMAS HOBBES

Peace: the soft and holy
shadow that virtue casts.

JOSH BILLINGS

We become the means of peace when we are willing to learn, to teach, to give, and especially to forgive.

FRANCES VAUGHAN
AND ROGER WALSH

When we do not find peace
within ourselves, it is vain
to seek for it elsewhere.

LA ROCHEFOUCAULD

A man of peace pulsates a new kind of energy into the world, he sings a new song. He lives in a totally new way, his very way of life is that of grace, that of prayer, that of compassion. Whomsoever he touches, he creates more love-energy. The man of peace is creative.

OSHO, FROM ZEN: THE PATH OF PARADOX, VOL. II

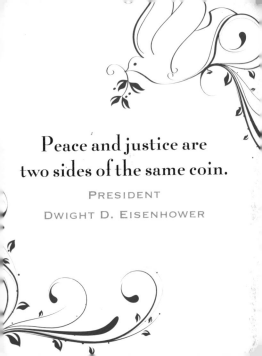

Peace and justice are
two sides of the same coin.

PRESIDENT
DWIGHT D. EISENHOWER

Peace of mind occurs
when our actions match
our beliefs.

IAN GAWLER

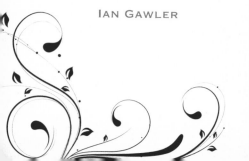

One day we must come to see that peace is not merely a distant goal we seek, but that it is a means by which we arrive at that goal. We must pursue peaceful ends through peaceful means.

DR. MARTIN LUTHER KING, JR.

First the mind has to be
quiet, control it, don't let
it wander, because when
you have a quiet mind
life is extraordinary.

J. KRISHNAMURTI

Go outside, sit down on some grass or dirt, . . . take a deep breath, filling up with the gift of air. Soon, you will feel your connection to wholeness, and you will know peace.

BARBARA DeANGELIS

We can never gain
any peace of mind until we
secure our own soul.

MARGARET CHASE SMITH

Peace of mind has nothing
to do with the external
world; it has only to do with
our connection with God.

GERALD JAMPOLSKY

Inner peace and love are
the greatest of God's gifts.

TETON SIOUX PROVERB

Have courage for the great
sorrows of life and patience for
the small ones; and when you
have laboriously accomplished
your daily task, go to sleep
in peace. God is awake.

VICTOR HUGO

We limit ourselves by thinking
that things can't be done.
Many think peace in the world
is impossible—many think that
inner peace cannot be attained.
It's the one who doesn't know
it can't be done who does it!

PEACE PILGRIM

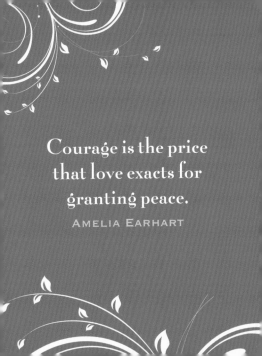

Courage is the price
that love exacts for
granting peace.

AMELIA EARHART

Peace is people talking
together with a heart
between them.

EIGHT-YEAR-OLD CHILD

Peaceful be earth, peaceful
heaven, peaceful waters, peaceful
trees . . . I render peaceful
whatever here is terrible,
whatever here is cruel,
whatever here is sinful.
Let it become auspicious,
let everything be beneficial to us.

HINDU PRAYER,
TENTH CENTURY BC

Be good to those who are good
And to those who are not.
For goodness increases goodness.
Have faith in those who are faithful
And in those who are not.
For faith brings greater faith
And goodness and faith build peace.

TAO 49

For Mercy has a human heart,
Pity a human face,
And Love, the human form
divine,
And Peace, the human dress.

WILLIAM BLAKE

Within the sphere of peace
there is no engine stronger
than love.

Climb the mountains and get
their good tidings. Nature's
peace will flow into you as the
sunshine flows into trees.
The winds will blow their
own freshness into you,
and the storms their energy,
while cares will drop off
like autumn leaves.

JOHN MUIR

Over all the mountain tops
is peace.

JOHANN WOLFGANG VON GOETHE

If there is to be peace on earth and good will toward man we must finally believe in the ultimate morality of the universe and believe that all reality hinges on moral foundations.

DR. MARTIN LUTHER KING, JR.

The true man of peace
rests in a peaceful mind.

ST. BONAVENTURE

Blessed are the peacemakers:
for they shall be called
the children of God.

MATTHEW 5:9 (KJV)

A man is in a state of peace
when he renders good for
good, as far as it lies in him
to do, and wishes harm
to no one.

BERNARD OF CLAIRVAUX

Little things seem nothing,
but they give peace, like those
meadow flowers which
individually seem odorless but
all together perfume the air.

GEORGES BERNANOS

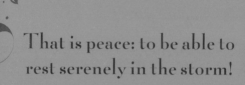

That is peace: to be able to
rest serenely in the storm!

DR. BILLY GRAHAM

To be able to see the world
in the light of love, which
can only come from within,
is to live without fear,
in unshakable peace.

DEEPAK CHOPRA

When we feel love
and kindness toward others,
it not only makes others feel
loved and cared for, but it
helps us also to develop
inner happiness and peace.

THE DALAI LAMA

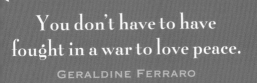

You don't have to have fought in a war to love peace.

GERALDINE FERRARO

Lord, make me an instrument of
Your peace. Where there is
hatred let me sow love;
where there is injury, pardon;
where there is doubt, faith;
where there is despair, hope;
where there is darkness, light;
and where there is sadness, joy.

ST. FRANCIS OF ASSISI

While conscience is our friend, all is at peace; however once it is offended, farewell to a tranquil mind.

LADY MARY WORTLEY MONTAGU

There is a wonderful mythical law of nature that the three things we crave most in life—happiness, freedom, and peace of mind—are always attained by giving them to someone else.

PEYTON CONWAY MARCH

When you make peace with
yourself, you make peace
with the world.

MAHA GHOSANANDA

Peace is available in
every moment, in every
breath, in every step.

People spend a lifetime searching for happiness; looking for peace. They chase idle dreams, addictions, religions, even other people, hoping to fill the emptiness that plagues them. The irony is the only place they ever needed to search was within.

RAMONA L. ANDERSON

Peace needs to be
in everyone's life.
The peace we are looking for
is within. It is in the heart,
waiting to be felt.

PREM RAWAT

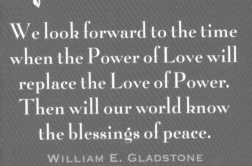

We look forward to the time when the Power of Love will replace the Love of Power. Then will our world know the blessings of peace.

WILLIAM E. GLADSTONE

We shall find peace.
We shall hear angels.
We shall see the sky
sparkling with diamonds.

ANTON CHEKOV

There never was a good war
or a bad peace.

BENJAMIN FRANKLIN

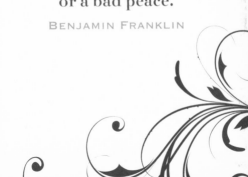

Here men from
the planet Earth first set
foot upon the Moon.
July 1969, A.D.
We came in peace
for all mankind.

TEXT OF PLAQUE ON MOON
LEFT BY APOLLO II MISSION

A crust eaten in peace
is better than a banquet
partaken in anxiety.

AESOP

Deep peace of the running wave
to you
Deep peace of the flowing air to you
Deep peace of the quiet earth to you
Deep peace of the shining stars to you
Deep joy of the leaping flame to you
Deep peace of the infinite peace
to you.

CELTIC BLESSING

Hope is like peace.
It is not a gift from God.
It is a gift only we can give
one another.

ELIE WIESEL

You can't separate peace
from freedom because no
one can be at peace unless
he has his freedom.

MALCOLM X

I want, of course, peace,
grace, and beauty.
How do you do that?
You work for it.

STUDS TERKEL

It is good to realize that if love and peace can prevail on earth, and if we can teach our children to honor nature's gifts, the joys and beauties of the outdoors will be here forever.

JIMMY CARTER

Work and live to serve
others, to leave the world
a little better than you
found it and garner for
yourself as much peace
of mind as you can.
This is happiness.

DAVID SARNOFF

If civilization is to survive,
we must cultivate the
science of human relation-
ships—the ability of all
peoples, of all kinds, to live
together, in the same
world at peace.

FRANKLIN D. ROOSEVELT

Be at peace with your own
soul, then heaven and earth
will be at peace with you.

ST. JEROME

One can not reflect in streaming water. Only those who know internal peace can give it to others.

LAO TZU

It is understanding that gives us an ability to have peace. When we understand the other fellow's viewpoint, and he understands ours, then we can sit down and work out our differences.

HARRY S. TRUMAN

Peace is rarely denied
to the peaceful.

FRIEDRICH SCHILLER

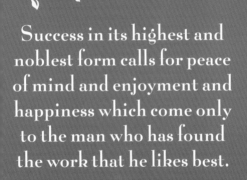

Success in its highest and noblest form calls for peace of mind and enjoyment and happiness which come only to the man who has found the work that he likes best.

NAPOLEON HILL

You cannot find peace
by avoiding life.

VIRGINIA WOOLF

Mother's love is peace.
It need not be acquired,
it need not be deserved.

ERICH FROMM

Until he extends his circle of compassion to include all living things, man will not himself find peace.

ALBERT SCHWEITZER

The great thing in the world
is not so much to seek
happiness as to earn peace
and self-respect.

THOMAS HUXLEY

Peace cannot be achieved through violence, it can only be attained through understanding.

ALBERT EINSTEIN

Peace begins with a smile.

MOTHER TERESA

For every minute you
remain angry, you give up
sixty seconds of
peace of mind.

RALPH WALDO EMERSON

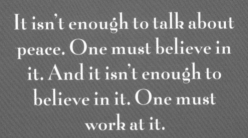

It isn't enough to talk about peace. One must believe in it. And it isn't enough to believe in it. One must work at it.

ELEANOR ROOSEVELT

It is a curious sensation:
the sort of pain that goes
mercifully beyond our powers
of feeling. When your heart is
broken, your boats are burned:
nothing matters any more.
It is the end of happiness and
the beginning of peace.

GEORGE BERNARD SHAW

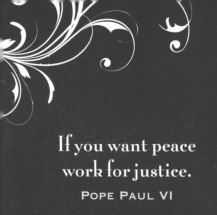

If you want peace
work for justice.

POPE PAUL VI

If everyone demanded peace
instead of another television
set, then there'd be peace.

JOHN LENNON

Each one has to find
his peace from within.
And peace to be real must
be unaffected by outside
circumstances.

MOHANDAS GANDHI

Peace is not absence of
conflict, it is the ability
to handle conflict by
peaceful means.

RONALD REAGAN

A mind at peace, a mind centered and not focused on harming others, is stronger than any physical force in the universe.

WAYNE DYER

Looking for peace is like looking for a turtle with a mustache: You won't be able to find it. But when your heart is ready, peace will come looking for you.

AJAHN CHAH,
REFLECTIONS